Yoga
For Stress

Monique Joiner Siedlak

OSHUN
PUBLICATIONS

Printed in the United States of America

Second Edition 2018

ISBN-13: 978-1-948834-66-7

Publisher
www.oshunpublications.com

Disclaimer
All the material contained in this book is provided for educational and informational purposes only. No responsibility can be taken for any results or outcomes resulting from the use of this material. While every attempt has been made to provide information that is both accurate and effective, the author does not assume any responsibility for the accuracy or use/misuse of this information.

Notice

This book is not intended as a substitute for the medical advice of physicians. The reader should regularly consult a physician or therapist in matters relating to his/her health and particularly with respect to any symptoms that may require diagnosis or medical attention.

Yoga Poses Photos

Pixabay.com

Freepik.com

Dreamstime.com

Cover Design by Monique Joiner Siedlak

Cover Image by Pixabay.com

Logo Design by Monique Joiner Siedlak

Logo Image by Pixabay.com

Sign up to email list: www.mojosiedlak.com

Other Books in the Series

Yoga for Beginners

Yoga for Back Pain

Yoga for Weight Loss

Yoga for Flexibility

Yoga for Advanced Beginners

Yoga for Fitness

Yoga for Runners

Yoga for Energy

Yoga for Your Sex Life

Yoga to Beat Depression and Anxiety

Yoga for Menstruation

Table of Contents

Introduction

Stress is unavoidable and can sneak its way into even the happiest person's life. Stress follows any ordeal that is characterized by our expectations or something we're working very hard for. It can raid our minds and bodies before weddings, examinations, presentations, social gatherings or just about even the most minor of things. Therefore, it's safe to say that being stressed is not our own choice, but in fact, it is a-free-of-cost feeling we get for every ordeal in our life as a spontaneous visitor.

Now that we're clear, stress comes and goes as it pleases but if it's getting too much, there are things we can do to avoid it for e.g. yoga. Here's how yoga helps to reduce stress:

Relaxes the Mind

It's all in your head/mind, which is why it's hard to get rid of it. Meditation will help that mind of yours to stop and focus on just one thing. There are certain yoga poses, which because of their complexity, help your mind to focus on them entirely, in turn, calming your brain that appears to be in a rut with all of the frantic thought processes.

Relaxes the Body

After the mind -comes the body. Yoga will help your body to release its tension and stress by breaking all barriers that had been holding all your muscles and nerves captive for so long. The different yoga poses will guide your body into various positions, resulting in increased flexibility and great posture. Whether your job had been a reason for stress for you or it was your personal life- yoga will help you focus on something that matters on hand.

Helps to Develop Connection of the Mind with the Body

Once you start doing yoga, your body will work to ease into all poses that you try. In doing so, your mind will come to terms with the requirement of concentration that the body will require from it. In no time your body and mind will work in perfect unison on the route to distressing.

Relaxed and Effective Breathing

Stress really affects the most trivial bodily functions as well as something as basic as breathing. If you are a stressed individual, you wouldn't even realize the parts of your mind and body the pent-up stress is affecting. Yoga will help to induce an 'everything's fine' and 'stay calm' feeling in you until your ragged breathing comes to a stable inhale and exhale. In this way, you'll realize How to Dough and anxious your breathing had been prior to beginning your yoga exercise.

Yoga is the best way to reduce all that pent-up stress, for a lot of reasons. It gives you the energy to release your emotions and directly and effectively with the least bit of damage to our own well-being. Just know that all of the stress, guilt, remorse, sadness, and anger resides inside our bodies. From shoulders to arms to legs to our backs, we store all the negativity from top to bottom. Yoga will help to let go of all of that and help us bury the hatchet with our own selves.

Now, let's get into the poses!

Mountain Pose (Tadasana)

The Mountain Pose can be employed as a resting pose or a preliminary pose for just about any standing asana. Even though this pose appears easy, it is great for improving your posture and body alignment, toning the spinal nerves, and creating a sense of consciousness throughout the body. As a pose in itself it's useful to practice. Simply stay in the pose for thirty seconds to one minute, breathing easily.

How to Do

Stand with the sides of your big toes coming into contact with each other. Your heels somewhat apart so that your second toes are matching. Elevate and expand your toes and the balls of your feet afterwards lay them gently down on the floor. Rock back and forth and side to side. Bit by bit decrease this move to and fro to a standstill, with your weight steadied equally on your feet.

Secure your thigh muscles and raise the kneecaps, without strengthening your lower belly. Raise the inside ankles to build up the inside arches. Begin to visualize a line of energy all the way up along your inner thighs to your groins, and from there through the core of your torso, neck, and head, and out through the top of your head. Turn the upper thighs somewhat inward. Elongate your tailbone in the direction of the floor and raise the pubis to the navel.

Pressing your shoulder blades into your back, broaden them crossways and drop them down towards your back. Without moving forward your lower front ribs, raise the top of your sternum straight toward the ceiling. Extend your collarbones, hanging your arms alongside your torso.

Square the top of your head straight over the middle of your pelvis, with the bottom of your chin parallel to the floor, throat soft, and the tongue wide and flat on the floor of your mouth. Soften your eyes.

Benefits

Improves posture, strengthens abdomen and buttocks. Can relieve back pain and decreases flat feet.

Tip

Use a block in the middle of the thighs. The block should be rotated so that the short end looks towards the front. With your legs, squeeze the block and roll it somewhat backward to feel the meeting and turning of the thighs. Take a number of breaths this way.

Then remove the block but replicate the action of your thighs as is the block was there. You don't have to use the block every time, but it helps to remember what rolling it back felt like.

Upward Hand Pose (Urdhva Hastasana)

Aimed at many individuals, the Upward Salute Pose is a relaxed way to stretch the entire body. Without most realizing it, this pose is regularly done spontaneously after sitting for long periods or sleeping.

How to Do

Standing in the Mountain Pose, breathe in while extending your arms first out to your sides and then over your head, with your fingers stretching up toward the ceiling.

Stretch your arms out from your body at the same time as slightly relaxing your shoulders down and away from your ears. Your legs will stay steadily fixed into the floor. Stretch throughout your fingertips, while inhaling and exhaling smoothly and deeply, taking your breath into the full length of your body.

Your eyes should be looking straight ahead or upward at about a forty-five-degree angle, keeping the sides of the neck extended, yet comfortable.

Benefits

Stretches your abdomen, while it also improves your digestion. Also, stretches your shoulders and armpits.

Tip

This pose should not be performed by individuals who may suffer from insomnia, headaches, or low blood pressure.

Eagle Pose (Garudasana)

The Eagle Pose might seem like a crazy yoga pose; however, it's not so difficult if you break it down. Because you pull your limbs into the body with the knees bent, your center of gravity is low. It is a stability challenge since it's less unstable than many poses where you're standing on one leg.

How to Do

Stand up straight. Bend your knees, lift your left foot and cross your left thigh over the right. Hook the top of the left foot behind the right calf. Stretch your arms to the sides parallel to the floor. Bend your elbows and raise your forearms perpendicular to the floor. Put your right elbow over your left elbow and press your palms together. Look straight.

Benefits

The Eagle Pose strengthens and stretches your ankles and calves while stretching the shoulders, upper back, thighs, and hips. It can improve concentration and your sense of balance.

Tip

If you have trouble balancing on one leg, this pose can be done in a chair to help you stay upright or rest your backside on a wall. Also, put a block under the foot if you can't hook the lifted foot around the calf.

Extended Hand to Big Toe Pose (Utthita Hasta Padangustasana)

Extended Hand to Big Toe Pose is an intermediary standing balancing pose.

How to Do

From mountain pose, shift your weight into your left leg. Reach your right hand on the inside of your right knee and take hold of your big toe with your first and second fingers. Firm the front thigh muscles of the standing leg, and press the outer thigh inward. You should rest here, finding your balance, then extend your foot forward. Straighten your knee fully if you can.

Keeping your leg straight, extend your foot towards the right. Keep your left hand on your left hip, or extend your hand out towards the left. Keep the shoulders level and relaxed away from the ears.

For the full appearance of this pose, direct your stare over your left shoulder, maintaining your chin parallel to the floor. Maintain this pose for fifteen to thirty seconds and at that time go back to Mountain Pose. Repeat this sequence on the other side.

Benefits

Improves leg strength, your sense of balance, core strength, and stretches the hamstrings.

Tip

You can hold this pose longer by supporting your raised-leg foot on the top side of a chair back which is padded with a blanket. Place the chair an inch or two away from the wall and push your elevated heel strongly to the wall.

Attempt utilizing a strap around the ball of your foot. After your hips and/or hamstrings are tight, you're not capable to straighten both legs while holding the big toe and maintaining your torso lifted. The strap will extend the length of your arm subsequently, and then you don't have to lift your leg as high, at the same time as still developing better flexibility in the pose.

Standing Forward Fold (Uttanasana)

Standing Forward Fold Pose is an important component of the Sun Salutations. This pose is used to train the body for deeper forward bends.

How to Do

Begin by Standing with your feet together. Bend your knees somewhat and bend your torso, not the lower back, over your legs, shift from your hips. Put your hands on the floor in front of you or next to your feet.

Breathe in and expand your chest to elongate your spine. Keep your focus fixed forward.

Breathe out and press both legs straight. Raise your kneecaps and twist your upper and inner thighs back. Without hyperextending, maintain your legs straight.

Extend your torso down without rounding your back, on an exhalation. Stay long through your neck, lengthening the top of your head toward the ground. Pull your shoulders down your back.

Benefits

The Standing Forward Fold pose extends your spinal column and stretches the back muscles as well as the backs of your legs.

Tip

Bend your knees to increase the stretch in the backs of your legs. Take care not to straighten the knees by locking them back; as an alternative, allow them to straighten as the two ends of each leg move farther spaced out.

Downward Facing Dog Pose (Adho Mukha Svanasana)

Downward Facing Dog Pose is one of the traditional Sun Salutation sequences poses. It's also an excellent yoga asana all on its own.

How to Do

Begin with your hands and knees in a tabletop position. Make sure your shoulders are aligned above your wrists and your hips are aligned above your knees. Come to a flat back by lengthening the spine. Place your head and neck in a non-aligned position, staring down in the direction of the floor.

Breathe out and raise your knees away from the floor. At the start, keep your knees slightly bent and your heels lifted away from the floor. Lengthen your tailbone positioned from the back of your pelvis and press it slightly toward the pubis. Alongside this tension, raise the resting bones in the direction of the ceiling, and from your inner ankles pull the inner legs up into the groin.

Followed by letting your breath out, push your top thighs back and extend your heels against or down toward the floor. Making sure that you do not lock them, straighten your knees and steady your outer thighs, rolling the upper thighs inward slightly, narrowing the front of the pelvis.

Firming the outer arms, press the bottoms of your index fingers assertively into the floor. From these two points, lift alongside the inside of your arms from the wrists to the tops of the shoulders. Firm your shoulder blades against your back then widen them and draw them toward the tailbone. Keep your head between your upper arms; not allowing it to simply hang.

Continue in this pose somewhere between one to three minutes. Afterward, bend your knees to the floor with a breath and repose in the Child's Pose.

Benefits

Downward Facing Dog pose can help decrease back pain through strengthening the whole back and shoulder girdle. It aids in stronger hands, wrists, the Achilles tendon, low-back, hamstrings, and calves, as well as increasing the full-body circulation. Elongates your shoulders and shoulder blade area. Decrease in tension and headaches by elongating the cervical spine and neck and relaxing the head. It can also lessen anxiety and expand your respiration

Tip

You can alleviate the burden on your wrists by employing a block beneath your palms or you can be capable of completing the pose upon your elbows. By lifting your hands on blocks or the seat of a chair, you can help to release and open your shoulders.

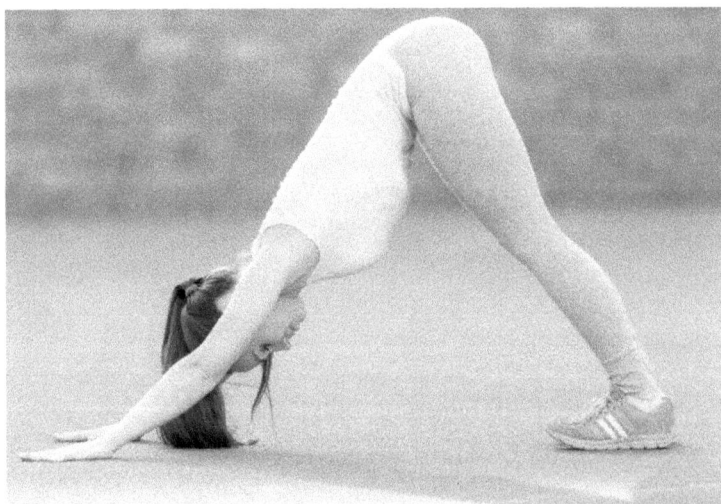

Upward Facing Dog Pose (Urdhva Mukha Svanasana)

Upward Facing Dog Pose is one of the most commonly known, as well as Downward Dog Pose, and recognized yoga pose due to its many benefits and healing uses. Similar to the Cobra Pose, it is thought of as one of the simplest of the back-bending poses and is implemented during the traditional Sun Salutation sequence.

How to Do

Lie face down on the floor. Stretch your legs back, with the tops of your feet on the floor. Bend your elbows and stretch your palms on the floor at the side of your waist so that your forearms are somewhat erect to the floor.

Breathe in and press your inner hands firmly into the floor and somewhat back, similar to trying to push yourself forward along the floor. Then at the same time, straighten your arms and lift your torso up and your legs a few inches off the floor on an intake breath. Keep the thighs firm and somewhat turned inward, the arms firm and turned out so the elbow creases face forward.

Press your tailbone toward your pubis and lift pubis toward your navel. Contract the hip positions. Stiffen but do not totally harden the buttocks.

Steady your shoulder blades against the back and puff the side ribs forward. Lift through the top of the sternum but make an effort not to push the front ribs forward. It will prompt the lower back to tighten. You will at that point look forward or you can angle your head towards the back slightly, remembering to take care not to constrict the back of your neck and the tightening of your throat.

Even though Upward Facing Dog Pose is one position used in the traditional Sun Salutation sequence, you can correspondingly practice this pose independently, maintaining the pose fifteen to thirty seconds, inhaling slowly. Release back to the floor or lift into the Downward Facing Dog pose along with an exhalation.

Benefits

Upward Facing Dog helps open the chest and strengthens the whole body and aligns the spine and invigorates nervous system and the kidneys.

Tip

Performing Upward Facing Dog will elongate and strengthen your whole body. You can use it as a backbend by itself, or as a transition for even deeper backbends.

Cobra Pose (Bhujangasana)

The Cobra Pose is a familiar Yoga backbend. When you perform the Cobra Pose, you stretch the front of your torso and spine.

How to Do

Lie face down on the floor. Extend your legs back, with the tops of your feet on the floor. Stretch your hands on the floor beneath your shoulders. Squeeze the elbows back into your body. Push the tops of your feet, thighs, and pubis powerfully into the floor.

On an inhalation, start to straighten your arms to raise your chest off the floor. Go only to a height at which you can sustain a connection throughout your pubis to your legs. Press your tailbone toward the pubis and raise the pubis toward your navel. Narrow the hip, compressing but don't harden your buttocks.

Firm the shoulder blades against the back, puffing the side ribs forward. Lift through the top of the sternum but avoid pushing the front ribs forward, which only hardens the lower back. Distribute the backbend evenly throughout the full spine.

Hold the pose anywhere from fifteen to thirty seconds, breathing freely. Release back to the floor with an exhalation.

Benefits

The Cobra Pose is best known for its capability to build up the flexibility of your spine. It stretches the chest along with strengthening your spine and shoulders. It further assists in opening the lungs and stimulating the abdominal organs, improving digestion.

An energizing backbend, the Cobra Pose can reduce stress and fatigue. It also firms and tones the shoulders, abdomen, and buttocks, and assists in easing back pain.

Tip

The Cobra Pose will be able to energize and warm up the body, getting it ready for the deeper backbends in your yoga routine.

Four-Limbed Staff Pose (Chaturanga Dandasana)

The Four-Limbed Staff Pose is also frequently known as the half-push up. When done correctly, your body resembles a staff or rod, with the spine in one straight line. It is a fundamental component of the Sun Salutations.

How to Do

Bringing your hands shoulder-width apart; supporting your shoulders, elbows, and wrists. Bend your arms straight back, keeping the upper arms hugging into your sides as you lower down toward the floor.

Engage your core and keep your hips raised up creating a line of energy from the crown of your head through your heels. Stop when your forearms and upper arms are at a right angle. So your shoulders are at the same level with your elbows. Hold the pose for ten to thirty seconds, taking four deep breaths. Release with an exhalation.

Benefits

The Four-Limbed Staff Pose tones and strengthens your abs. Builds muscle upper arms, back, and shoulders and wrists.

Tip

For beginners, bring your knees to the floor until you can build enough strength to hold your body up with the arms.

Keep in mind that your neck remains balanced. Your eyes are to the floor. Allowing your body to lower below your elbows can cause elbow strain. If you have wrist conditions, for instance, carpal tunnel syndrome, you should avoid this pose.

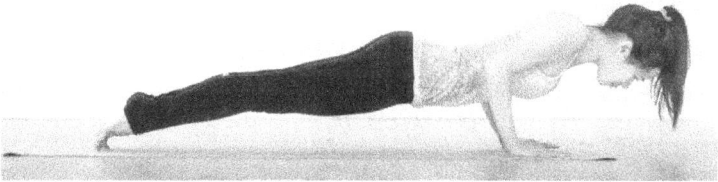

Bridge Pose (Setu Bandha Sarvangasana)

The Bridge Pose is a beginning backbend that helps to open your chest and stretch your thighs.

How to Do

To begin, lie supine (on your back). Fold your knees and keep your feet hip distance apart on the floor, ten to twelve inches from your pelvis, with your knees and ankles in a straight line. With your arms beside your body, place your palms faced down.

Breathe in, while slowly lifting your lower back, middle back and upper back off the floor. Gently roll in your shoulders. Touch your chest to your chin without bringing the chin down. Support your weight with your shoulders, arms, and feet. Feel your buttocks firm up in this pose. Both your thighs should be parallel to each other and to the floor.

You could interlock your fingers and push your hands on the floor to lift your torso a bit more up if you want or you could support your back with your palms. Keep breathing easily.

Hold this pose for a minute or two and then exhale as you gently release the pose.

Benefits

The Bridge Pose strengthens your back, opens the chest, and improves your spinal mobility.

Tip

After you roll your shoulders under, be sure not to pull them away from your ears. This often overstrains your neck. Raise the tops of your shoulders toward your ears and push your inner shoulder blades away from your spine.

Legs up The Wall Pose (Viparita Karani)

The Legs up the Wall Pose is an upturn pose where you lie on the floor against a wall and position your legs together vertically against the wall.

How to Do

If you are performing the assisted version, place a firm pillow or cushion on the floor against the wall.

Start off the pose by sitting with your right side against the wall. Your lower back should rest against the bolster if you're using one. Slightly turn your body to the right and bring your legs up onto the wall. On the other hand, if you are using a pillow, shift your lower back onto it before bringing your legs up the wall. Use your hands for balance as you transfer your weight.

Drop your back to the floor and lie down. Relax your shoulders and head on the floor. Transfer your weight from side-to-side and move your buttocks close to the wall. Allow your arms to rest open at your sides with your palms facing up. If you're using a pillow, your lower back should at this time be totally held by it.

Allow the part of your bone that connects in the hip socket (the top of your thigh bones) to release and relax, dropping in the direction of the back of your pelvis.

Close your eyes and hold for five to ten minutes, as you breathe with mindfulness.

To release, slowly boost yourself away from the wall and slide your legs down to the left side. Use your hands to help press yourself back up into a seated position.

Benefits

This pose reduces fatigue, cramping in the legs and feet and stretches the back of the legs. It can be an excellent pose for alleviating swollen ankles and calves triggered by long periods of standing pregnancy, and travel. It furthermore elongates the front of the upper body as well as the back of the neck and can be helpful for relieving mild backaches.

Tip

Use your breath to ground the tops of your thighs bones into the wall, which assists in the release of your abdomen, spine, and groins. Imagine in the pose, which each inhalation is falling through your upper body and pushing the tops of your thigh bones closer to the wall. Next with each exhale, hold your thighs to the wall and let your upper body extend over the bolster away from the wall and onto the floor.

Head-To-Knee Forward Bend Pose (Janu Sirsasana)

The Head-to-Knee Forward Bend Pose is a deep, forward bend that soothes the mind and releases stress. It is frequently practiced near the end of a sequence, when the body is warm, to set up the body for even deeper forward bends.

How to Do

Start in a seated pose with your legs stretched. Bend the right leg, pulling the bottom of the foot to the upper inside of the right thigh. The right knee must rest steadily on the floor. Take both hands to both sides of the left leg. Breathe in and turn towards your extended leg. Breathe out and fold forward. Exhale slowly and deeply for three to five breaths. To come out of the pose, breathe in back to the beginning position. Repeat the other side.

Benefits

Helps tone your legs and burn the fats in your abdominal.

Tip

You can sit up on a blanket if your hips are tight. Place a strap about the extended foot, If you like or hold an end of the strap in each hand as you forward bend.

Child's Pose (Balasana)

The Child's Pose is a popular beginner's yoga posture. It is generally utilized as a resting position in among more difficult poses throughout a yoga practice.

How to Do

Come to all fours (Table Pose) exhale and lower your hips to your heels and forehead to the floor. Kneeling on the floor, bring your big toes together and sit on your heels, then separate your knees about as far as your hips.

Your arms can be above your head with your palms on the floor. Your palms can be flat or fisted with them stacked under your forehead, or your arms can be at the sides of your body with your palms up.

The Child's Pose is a resting pose. Remain in this position anywhere from thirty seconds to a few minutes. Beginners can also use this pose to get a feel of a deep forward bend. To come up, first stretch your front torso, followed by an inhalation lift from your tailbone as it pushes down and into your pelvis.

Benefits

The Child's Pose aids to stretch your hips, thighs, and ankles at the same time it reduces stress and fatigue. It gradually relaxes the muscles on the front of your body while softly and reflexively elongates the muscles of the back of your torso.

As it centers, calm, and soothes your brain, the Child's Pose is said to be a beneficial posture for alleviating stress. When done with your head and torso braced, it can as well help relieve back and neck pain.

The Child's Pose soothes the body, mind, and spirit while stimulating your third eye. Gently stretching the lower back, the Child's Pose massages and tones your abdominal organs, and encourages digestion and elimination.

Tip

Before you relax completely, press your palms into the ground with your arms straight and elbows lifted. Push your hips firmly back toward your heels. Breathe deeply into your whole back, for an extra release in your back. Make use of this pose to rest in the middle of more challenging poses.

Corpse Pose (Shavasana)

The Corpse Pose is typically performed at the end of a yoga sequence. It can on the other hand be utilized at the start to calm your body before performing or in the midpoint of a sequence to rest. When applied at the conclusion of a yoga practice it is usually followed by a seated meditation phase to re-incorporate the body mind spirit back into the world.

How to Do

Lying on your back let your arms and legs drop open. With your arms at about forty five degrees from the side of your body, make sure you are comfortable and warm. With your eyes closed begin with slow deep breaths through the nose.

Allowing your entire body to become soft and heavy, let it relax onto the floor. As your body relaxes, feel your full body expanding and decreasing with each breath. Glance over your body from your toes to the top of your head, inspecting for any tension, stiffness or tightened muscles. Intentionally let go and relax any spots that you may find. Sway or shake those parts of your body from side to side to boost further release.

Let go of all control of your breath, your mind, and your body. Allow your body to move deeper and further into a state of complete relaxation. Remain in the Corpse Pose for five to fifteen minutes.

To release the Corpse Pose gradually deepen your breath, wriggle your fingers and toes, bring your arms over your head and stretch your entire body, breathing out, bend your knees into your chest, then roll over to one side going into the fetal position. Once you are ready, slowly inhaling, rising up into a seated position.

Benefits

The Corpse Pose allows your body and mind the time to sort out what has occurred during a yoga session. To most individuals, no yoga session is finished without this final pose. Your body needs this time to comprehend the new information it has received during the practice of yoga. Even though the Corpse Pose is a resting pose, you are not going to sleep.

Tip

Simply, relax. Follow your breathing without striving to control it. Observe what's taking place in your body. Gather your thoughts as they come along and let them go.

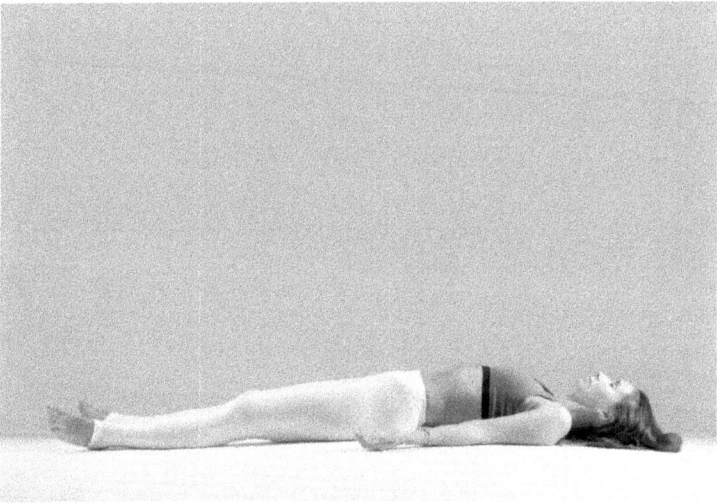

Constructing a Yoga Sequence

Here are a few points to keep in mind how to construct a yoga sequence. You are not at a studio, paying to be there. You do not have to exercise for over an hour. Begin with 5-10 minutes. Notice how you feel by the end of this time. If you feel as if you can do more, go ahead. If no, end your routine there.

Start with 5-10 minutes. By the conclusion of that time, notice how you feel. Do you desire to resume? If yes, continue for an extra five minutes and then check in with yourself once more. If not, close your workout.

The same as any physical journey, a yoga sequence has three clear parts.

Your opening or warm-up sequence

You don't want to jump into the main event tight and cold. This is where you move through and loosening up your major muscle groups as well as body parts

Your main sequence

Once you've warmed up, it's time for your main sequence. This component of your sequence is influenced by the goal of your routine. If it's an asymmetrical pose, keep in mind to do both sides and devote about the same time on each side.

The closing or cool down sequence

Now you've completed the principal portion of your yoga practice, it's time to cool down.

About The Author

Monique Joiner Siedlak is a writer, witch, and warrior on a mission to awaken people to their greatest potential through the power of storytelling infused with mysticism, modern paganism, and new age spirituality. At the young age of 12, she began rigorously studying the fascinating philosophy of Wicca. By the time she was 20, she was self-initiated into the craft, and hasn't looked back ever since. To this day, she has authored over 35 books pertaining to the magick and mysteries of life. Her most recent publication is book one of an Urban Paranormal series entitled "Jaeger Chronicles."

Originally from Long Island, New York, Monique is now a proud inhabitant of Northeast Florida; however, she considers herself to be a citizen of Mother Earth. When she doesn't have a book or pen in hand, she loves exploring new places and learning new things. And being the nature lover that she is, she considers herself to be an avid animal advocate.

To find out more about Monique Joiner Siedlak artistically, spiritually, and personally, feel free to visit her official website, **www.mojosiedlak.com**.

Other Books by Monique Joiner Siedlak

Mojo's Wiccan Series

Wiccan Basics

Candle Magick

Wiccan Spells

Love Spells

Abundance Spells

Hoodoo

Herb Magick

Seven African Powers: The Orishas

Moon Magick

Cooking for the Orishas

Creating Your Own Spells

Body Mind and Soul Series

Creative Visualization

Astral Projection for Beginners

Meditation for Beginners

Reiki for Beginners

Thorne Witch Series

The Phoenix

Beautiful You Series

Creating Your Own Body Butter

Creating Your Own Body Scrub

Creating Your Own Body Spray

Mojo's Self-Improvement Series

Manifesting With the Law of Attraction

Stress Management

Jaeger Chronicles

Glen Cove

Connect With Me!

I really appreciate you reading my book! Please leave a review and let me know your thoughts. Here are the social media locations you can find me at:

Like my **Facebook Page:** www.facebook.com/mojosiedlak

Follow me on **Twitter:** www.twitter.com/mojosiedlak

Follow me on **Instagram: www.**instagram.com/mojosiedlak

Follow me on **Bookbub:** http://bit.ly/2KEMkqt

Sign up to my **Email List** at www.mojosiedlak.com and receive a free book!

If you enjoyed this book or found it useful I'd be very grateful if you'd post a short review on at your retailer. Your support really does make a difference and I read all the reviews personally so I can get your feedback and make this as well as the next book even better.

www.ingramcontent.com/pod-product-compliance
Lightning Source LLC
Chambersburg PA
CBHW071633040426
42452CB00009B/1598